Bud the cub is in the bus.
Gus the cub is in the bus.
Dad is glad.

2 Dad tells Bud and Gus
not to miss the bus back.

3

4

Bud and Gus miss the bus.
Bud is sad and Gus is sad.
But Dad is mad!

Bud and Gus run.
Bud falls!
Gus tugs Bud.

6

Dad has a big lap.
Bud the cub is glad.
Gus the cub is glad.

The cubs are in a jam!

How can you be on time?